Write and Direct Your Feature Film

Tom Kennerly

DEDICATION

The brave, alas, will not live forever.
But the timid and the cautious may not live at all...

CONTENTS

Acknowledgements

I didn't realize how easy my life was until I decided to become a 'film maker'. Since the day that I fell out of the normal tree and smacked my head against every branch on the way down, I have confused loved ones with my dogged persistence. I beg their forgiveness; I must persist.

Funny thing about repeatedly banging your head;

It sure opens your eyes.

ONE

Make a movie. I mean, why not?

Personally, I had all of the typical American dreams with respect to my future vocation. Cowboy, point guard, and motocross champion were the more dominant. It was much later in life that I got the feeling that hanging out with starlets as I strutted across the movie set would be a cool job, and lo and behold, it happened.

The starlets don't pay much attention to me, and I don't do much strutting(anymore), but I have met some fantastic, creative people, and made movies with them, and seen myself on the silver screen along with them. It hasn't sucked.

Due to my unique perspective on independent film making, I've published a small array of videos and books, and done some blogging, to try to put the things I've learned out there in the hopes that a few more folks can live the dream. It is to those ends that I offer this little jewel.

There is something really special when I know that a creation, all my own is making its way from my foggy brain through to the ends of my fingertips - when I know that a great story idea is there, and a few painstaking hours at the keyboard will translate those raw thoughts into a blue print that, just maybe, will become a feature film.

Can everyone do it? Probably. Can everyone do it well? Probably not. But it sure the heck is worth a try.

What's different about this book?

Very important. If you don't like what it is I have to say, or the way in which I say it, you can make your way to the internet and buy two books – one, a book about the correct way to format your screenplay, and, two, a book about the way you should 'develop' your screenplay. Characterization, and all that other stuff.

You can tell that I'm not of that bend. The correct format is EXTREMELY important, and I'll discuss that later. But - and if you get this through your head, you will be out in front of a lot of overpaid people in southern California – screenplays aren't movies.

Screenplays aren't movies.

The screenplay is an all important roadmap, and foundation, for a project that will culminate in a film. That FILM should have compelling characters, and an arc, and three acts, and all the other things that people you have never heard of want to preach to you about in their how-to books. You know why you've never heard of them? Because they've probably never made a feature film that has made it into distribution.

This book...

...is for folks who want to get a great idea onto paper and whip it into a screenplay that they intend to put to use on a low or no budget project. If you have the notion of 'selling' a screenplay, you may want to buy one of those books I just described. Selling a screenplay is a bit like winning an argument with your Mother. You hear that it has happened, and that it probably will happen again, but it never seems to happen to you. I have films in distribution worldwide, and **I've** never sold a screenplay. I don't want to. I want to make movies. I hope you do, too.

I'm not going to tell you how to produce, or 'make' a movie in this book, just to be clear, We will, however, discuss how the decisions we make about our screenplay's formation will help or hinder our project in the production stage.

Ready? Let's go.

ONE AND A HALF

As the 'number' of this chapter suggests, I wasn't quite sure where this chapter best fit. Hopefully, you will endeavor to persevere, and type 'the end' a hundred or so pages into your unique vision, visit these pages again, and then start making a movie.

The number one reason that I threw together this particular group of thoughts is; if you can finish your screenplay, there has NEVER been a better time to see your movie come to life. DSLR cameras costing under $1000 have been used to shoot films which have grossed millions of dollars, digital editing packages are so affordable and feature rich that studios now use the digital intermediate process, turning film into digital files, editing them, then turning them *back* into film prints. (and ironically, then BACK into digital files and delivered to theaters via hard drive, in the case of those theaters who have been able to convert to digital projectors)

Will your no or low budget film have the same production value as a studio project, or even a million dollar indie? No. But...

Distribution is very, very, different now.

I can't believe the proliferation of tablets. Also, I'm knocked out by those, (like me) who no longer have a standalone DVD player in their living room. Film Festivals have gone online. There are so many different ways to exhibit your film, that preparing it for possible theatrical exhibition is no longer a concern. (it never really should have been for a first or second project, but that's another book) My point is, you are NOT writing this screenplay with the feeling of pitching a penny into a fountain. Anyone with a little energy and guts can now go to his or her own premiere.

In any earlier paragraph you'll note that I mentioned the conversion to digital projectors. Put up with a little back-story here, and you will leave with one more warm and fuzzy feeling about your chances in the movie distribution game.

For the pretty much the whole twentieth century, theaters received film in cans, assembled them, most of the time in the correct order, and showed them for the duration of the film's 'run'. they would then pass the film back to the distributor – or onto the 'second run' theater, who would probably charge a little less for this slightly older release. This feature film print, weighing approximately 65 pounds, was shipped and couriered around during its travels. It was usually insured and accounted for very closely, as in the year 2000 the approximate cost to manufacture a film print was between $1500 and $2000 dollars.

Now. a typical nationwide release of a film involves a 2500 or more theaters. 2500 theaters times $2000 ? *Five million dollars just for film prints.* There is a term in the film game called P and A, prints and advertising. So, you get XYZ company to take on your film for a theatrical release. If you GIVE it to them, they have to invest all that money just for prints, (we haven't even talked about ht cost of advertising) Do you see why it has always been such a challenge for indie features to get theatrical releases?

But now...the film is loaded onto an everyday hard drive (usually used) which weighs less than a pound. It is loaded onto the digital projector, and in many cases the same drive is then shipped to another theater in the same week. Technology has taken the P in P and A down to almost nothing. One more hurdle removed for indie film makers on any budget.

Brief note, you see why distributors can't wait for a complete change over to digital...no doubt about it.

TWO

Nary a person who has been to the movies has not at one time or another thought to him or herself; 'that would make a great movie'. I sure have. The reason that all of those folks haven't made a movie is that 'ideas for a movie' are worth squat. I hate to be so serious, but moving a kernel of an idea through a writing process, and then moving that result (the screenplay) through the production process, is what makes movies. A LOT of this work is tedious, and it takes time. I, however, will offer you a few options when it comes to 'the process'. One of these should make you feel as if you are making progress, and inspire you to sweat just a little more over the keyboard.

But; no keyboard yet. First, let's grab a legal pad or notebook and sketch out some thoughts.

The Kernel

More than one of my stories has been inspired by just one particular scene that has developed in my head. So I write it out, and describe the details - including the characters and locations. I let it sit for a day or so, and the thoughts of those characters; who they are, what got them to that scene, and what they might do after that scene, can easily inspire other scenes. However your mind works, I encourage you to give this approach a try, because, it's fun!

The Three Acts

No matter your approach, if you want your project to have a snowball's chance in Hades, you will have to whip it into three acts sooner or later. You may not realize it, but as a consumer, you've been conditioned into three act features that are about an hour and forty five minutes long. Want to break new ground? Want to be different? Go read somebody else' book. For the purpose of distribution you need a movie that fits 'the norm'.

This approach works well if you feel that you know the 'plot' of your movie, but not the details. So, this approach will have you divide a page into three sections. Mark them first, second, and third act. Then start filling in the different plot points, the twists and turns of your plot. The closer you are to having an even amount of 'points' down your page, the closer you are to having an idea that can be told in approximately one hundred and five minutes. It is very common to have beginning points and end points, but not enough middle. That's okay. Better to know that now, not later. There are films that make it to the movie theater that don't know that they're missing too much middle...or in industry speak, have 'no second act'.

The Skeleton

Similar to 'the three acts' approach, but this is for a situation where you may not be sure of the plot, but you know the type of film that you would like to make. Some very successful writers in many areas of publishing let the keyboard guide their plot, and I'll go so far as to say that this approach may be the most creative. Downside: it's also a bit risky; as this method will allow you to write yourself into the proverbial corner.

THREE

*The Asterisk Chapter

I flipped a coin, and decided to include this short chapter in an effort to let you, the reader, make an informed choice with respect to your (I hope) ultimate goal of seeing your screenplay up there on the screen. It is not meant to censor your dreams or desires.

That being said:

There is a way to increase the likelihood of your film making it into distribution *one hundred fold* right here at the outset, and that is to write a certain type of script. It's not science fiction. It's not action. It's not buddy cop. No, not romantic comedy either. It's called Ten Little Indians.

Ten Little Indians: A group of some sort, gets to a destination of some sort, and makes a wrong turn of some sort, that has them get picked off systematically by a nemesis of some sort, until one of them makes a stand of some sort.

It's been done a thousand times.

It has sold billions of dollars of tickets, rentals, and consumables. Does this limit you to horror or thriller? Probably. But that's a fairly wide playing field. Horror doesn't have to be wall to wall blood, or it can be, if that's what you choose. Anyway, write what you want, but I've spoken my piece.

In the book world, there's fiction and non-fiction. In the movie world, we call it documentary and **narrative.** Why? I don't know. The point is, scripts are for narratives. Documentaries are a whole other animal, which, I can't speak to. I would hope you haven't come this far without that point being clear. It is now...

FOUR

Screenwriter's Tip – No Bar Scenes!

Yes, yes, much time is spent in our formative years treading the hoppy smelling boards of bars. It makes sense that when letting our imaginations run supposedly wild, we picture the leading man and woman doing various screen-worthy things in 'a bar'. Here's why you want to avoid that. Bars make money almost every day of the year. In general, there's no time to shoot. Also, bars are full of stuff that gets consumed and or goes missing when a dozen people, most of whom the owner doesn't know, are allowed to mill around in it, unsupervised. I know what you're thinking. Favorite bar owner #1 likes me! He'll let me. And if not, Favorite *bartender* #1 up the street likes me. He'll ask the owner of his...

Please, listen up. You will set yourself up for disappointment with these scenarios. An exception of course, is if your favorite uncle owns the place, and he isn't just pretending to like you.

This example is something that needs to be considered for ALL of the exotic locations that cross your mind. A film cast and crew, even a micro budget one, is a travelling circus. Allowing someone to come in and shoot is a helluva favor. Think about that now if you really are planning to make this movie.

So, on with the chapter.

One of the ways that I know that I have a story that will make it 90 minutes on my hands, is the number of plot points that accumulate within the three acts dividing up my piece of notebook paper in a very balanced way. Examples of plot points:

- Sheena and Jim have their first fight

- Jim returns to pick up his paycheck

- Sheena goes into the basement to investigate a sound

As you see, these are small scene summaries. In my mind, they are an 'invitation' to begin writing that scene. But, at this point, if you have seven of these in each of the three acts, you have a pretty good foundation. Other scenes will find their way into your screenplay as you flesh out the original scenes you pictured, as the smaller scenes require linking and setting up. Also, writing scenes that you have already conceived of will inspire other scenes as the characters and locations become more vivid in your mind, as I alluded to earlier.

FIVE

The Seven Stories

This subject works, as they say, on 'many levels'. It is a basic tenet of writing which says that there really are only seven different stories that have been, and ever will be written. (You can find arguments out there ranging from twenty-six, down to one in this area, but let's go with the popular seven for now) Meaning, seven basic plots.

You're new to story writing (or you probably wouldn't be reading this book), so you really, really need to lay out a typical plot. You've consumed many, many movies over the years, you know the makings as well as the pace, of a typical plot. Those descriptions with words like 'denouement' aren't very interesting. Here's the way I like to pace my stories.

- Intro

- Uh-oh

- More trouble

- MORE TROUBLE

- HOLY CRAP!

- Hero prevails

Screenwriter's tip – flashbacks and forwards should be rare, if at all.

What does this have to do with the seven stories? Over the course of developing your screenplay you will need to find a pace and rhythm which will keep your audience engaged and unconfused. The relatively equal acts, and my sequential trouble formula will do that. Skipping around the planet, through time, and in other ways, will not.

Shifting gears for a moment – note that we haven't actually started a screenplay, or script. That's good! Anyone can type FADE IN. Not everyone knows where they're going when they do so. The confidence that you feel when YOU type FADE IN, knowing that your noggin holds a great scene, or character, or plot point, is rewarding enough to help you stay with it when it turns to 'work'.

And it will.

SIX

This chapter will focus on something that I don't like in particular, but if you and I put this tool to use more often, we will increase our chances of making great movies. This something is:

The Treatment

A treatment is a descriptive, un-dramatic summary of your screenplay. I usually force myself into writing my treatment after the screenplay is finished, for marketing and other production oriented purposes. This is bad. Bad, bad, bad. Why? Because we can put this treatment to use in determining if our story is lopsided, short, long, or just not going anywhere.

Treatments can be as short as a paragraph, or as long as twenty typewritten pages, but a very common length is a page and one half.

A Sample Treatment:

Sheena and Jim rent a rambling old home in a small northeastern town. They are quickly comfortable with the home and the small town. Jim finds a job, and Sheena begins housekeeping in an old fashioned way.

Soon, Sheena is almost unwilling to leave
the house. Questions of 'where their
relationship is going' begin driving Jim
away, and find Sheena seeking comfort only
within their home. Several times she is
about to leave, and a distraction occurs,
and she does not. (Example: On pulling shut
the front door, the old lockset refuses to
latch. Not wanting to leave the house
unlocked, Sheena digs out tools, and changes
to more comfortable clothes, and by the time
the lock is in working order, it's time to
start dinner)

After confronting Sheena with his
perspective on her problem, Sheena reacts
violently, and avoids him. Soon, the house
does the same. At one point, Jim's foot
breaks through an old wooden step, the
splintered wood gashing his leg causing a
bloody wound.

While being tended to at the local walk in

medical center, the receptionist recalls
that the house had a rich history, and Jim
investigates online, finding that a young
boy went missing a century ago, and Jim and
Sheena's home is listed as his address at
the time.

Jim contacts his amateur ghost hunter friend
from the big city, and after a few false
starts, the hunter is drawn to the backyard.
In a wild storm, Jim and the ghost hunter
dig. They find the plaster pit common with
turn of the century home construction, and
within it, the clothes of a five year old
boy draped on a tiny skeleton. Years ago,
having not heeded warnings from the workmen,
the boy had fallen in.

Some Notes

As you can see, this is void of and flair or drama. That's what
makes it had for writers to write. One need to force himself to
skip over important plot points and transitions. However, once
you knock this together, you really start to think about the
requirements of your script. Having the right house to shoot in is

half the battle in this example, right?

To follow my 'uh-uh formula', we would have Jim be injured more than once, and have Sheena be distracted several times. Where did they move from? Where does Jim work?

Important for the SCRIPT, but not for this treatment. There is a beginning, crisis, and end, and some juicy scenes can be hung from it.

Selling

Also, I like to finish my scripts before I recruit cast and crew, but that doesn't mean that you have to. A treatment of the length above could be used to attract early interest from some of the folks that you have in mind that would be key to the production.

Finally, when you get to the distribution stage of the project, potential distributors, as well as your chosen distributor, will probably ask you for a treatment to help with their marketing. You'll already have one.

SEVEN

This chapter will cover another piece that shows good planning on your part if you attack it before actually starting your script and this piece is the Character Summary, or Character Breakdown. My example:

```
Jim - 30, an old soul, world worn for his
years.  Average build, covered mostly in
jeans and a t-shirt.

Sheena - 25, tall and dark, trying
desperately to play the simple hand life has
dealt her.  She and Jim have been together
about three years.

Vince - 30, jack of all trades, including
ghost hunting.  Continually riding the
border of amiable and obnoxious.
```

Probably the way that things will work out is that you will start your character breakdown with the main, or principle characters fairly well, described and then add others as the story takes shape. that's great.

One of the primary reasons for getting these descriptions on paper is for *you* to know who these people are as the script takes shape. If you find yourself typing 'long cool blonde' or 'boy next door' for the third time, you probably don't have a very diversified cast of characters. Also, you had better be able to find yourself a long cool blonde who can act.

Finally, it is a common freshman writing mistake to lean toward the cliché, as we all are in love with certain great characters from the movies.

```
Illinois Smith - 40, beat up leather hat,
bullwhip, and hates Nazis.
```

Sound a little too close to someone you know? You get the idea. The breakdown will help you see that you need to create your own characters. That's what this whole process is about.

EIGHT

Alright, I think it's time to start writing your script. Most of you reading this will be able to look at any sample script, and just by mimicking the style, start banging away. The next few chapters are just here to help you with some common details. Let's look over our example:

```
INT. JIM'S KITCHEN - DAY

JIM, 30, world-worn, rustles the paper as he
drinks his coffee.

                    JIM
                (mumbling)
          So, the Eagles lost again.

Jim rattles the paper some more.  He takes
a sip of coffee, and looks at the clock.

                    JIM(CNT'D)
                (shouting)
          It's eight o'clock, Sheena!

SHEENA, 25, a sleepy, tall brunette, glides
into the kitchen, and stops at the coffee
pot.
```

                    SHEENA
              (choking up)
       You used to make enough coffee
       for the both of us.

Sheena whips the coffee pot against the far
wall, where it explodes with a CRASH and
TINKLE of glass.

Sheena storms out of the kitchen and slams
the bedroom door on Jim. She screams at the
top of her lungs, as Jim simply shakes his
head.

                    SHEENA(O.S.)
              I hate you!

INT. JIM'S BEDROOM - DAY

Sheena is sobbing into her pillow

                    JIM(V.O.)
              I walked down to the drugstore
              for more smokes, and let her
              cry it out. Dames.

That's it. If you can imitate what you see above, and string scenes
like this together in a logical way, you will have a script. No, it's
not so hard.

So, I'm going to 'mark up' this script, and describe the formatting basics.

`INT. JIM'S KITCHEN - DAY` (This is a slug line. Interior or exterior, specific location, and night or day)

`JIM, 30, world-worn, rustles the paper as he drinks his coffee.`(This is the action. The first time that we mention a character in a script, we capitalize it, and give a brief description of that character)

                    `JIM` (Character about to speak, caps)
               `(mumbling)` (how the line is spoken)
          `So the Eagles lost again.`(dialogue)

Note the alignment for the above. Script software will align these for you. If you're using a word processor, you tab in to the respective alignments which you see here, the slug line starting one tab (five spaces) in.

`Jim rattles the paper some more.  He takes a sip of coffee, and looks at the clock.`

                    `JIM(CNT'D)`
               `(shouting)`
          `It's eight o'clock, Sheena!`

`SHEENA, 25, a sleepy, tall brunette, glides into the kitchen, and stops at the coffee pot.`

                    SHEENA
                (choking up)
        You used to make enough coffee
        for the both of us.

Sheena whips the coffee pot against the far
wall, where it explodes with a CRASH and
TINKLE of glass. (sound effects are capitalized)

Sheena storms out of the kitchen and slams
the bedroom door on Jim. She screams at the
top of her lungs, as Jim simply shakes his
head.

                    SHEENA (O.S.) (off screen)
            I hate you!

INT. JIM'S BEDROOM - DAY

Sheena is sobbing into her pillow

                    JIM (V.O.) (Voice over. Jim is not in the
room)
            I walked down to the drugstore
            for more smokes, and let her
            cry it out. Dames.

                                    FADE
                                (transition)

At first, there is a lot to learn, and looking back, I probably should have purchased some scriptwriting software when I first started. It's not that expensive, and it will speed your process, AND give you some neato reporting, like breakdowns. I currently use this type of software, but, my first two film distribution deals were based on scripts that I hammered out in plain old word processing software. The choice is an economic one, and it is all yours.

Sound effects are an inexpensive way to really increase the production value of an indie, so you should be conscious of their possibilities at the writing stage, as opposed to leaving them to chance in post production. You see how easy they are to 'write up'.

Voice over and Off Screen are going to appear in almost every screenplay out there so let's get them down, as they are similar but different. Off screen means that the character is 'in the scene', but out of the frame in this shot. In this example, Sheena has simply walked from the kitchen into the bedroom. she could even be in the same room, but out of the camera's frame, or, off screen. The example where Jim delivers voice over, you see that he is narrating, 'from the future'. You see this in movies when someone is reading a letter and the audio is in the writer's voice. A general rule is that voice over is from a character in a different time or place.

A few more common tools

Let's add some dialogue to our story, to showcase these examples:

```
INT.  JIM'S KITCHEN - NIGHT

Sheena and Jim look at their hands as they
sit across from each other at the kitchen
table.

                SHEENA
        I'm sorry, Jim, I shouldn't have...

                JIM
            (stepping on)
        No, no, it was my fault.


Sheena and Jim stretch their hands across
the table, and both smile as they hold each
others hands tightly.

INSERT - Jim's cellphone VIBRATES on the
kitchen table.

                                    (cnt'd)
BACK TO SCENE

                SHEENA
        Oh boy, I know who that is.
```

FADE

Alright let's mark it up:


```
INT.   JIM'S KITCHEN - NIGHT

Sheena and Jim look at their hands as they
sit across from each other at the kitchen
table.

                    SHEENA
        I'm sorry, Jim, I shouldn't have...

                    JIM
              (stepping on) (he cuts her off)
        No, no, it was my fault.


Sheena and Jim stretch their hands across
the table, and both smile as they hold each
others hands tightly.

INSERT - Jim's cellphone VIBRATES on the
kitchen table. (the editor will cut away to a shot of the
vibrating cell phone)
                    (scene continues to next page) (cnt'd)
BACK TO SCENE(the editor will return to the scene from the
insert)
```

```
                    SHEENA
        Oh boy,  I  know  who  that  is.


                                        FADE
```

Hot tip for 'stepping on', give your first speaker enough dialogue to
BE stepped on. I'm sorry... doesn't give Jim much to step on, does
it? You see here that we've written just a bit more. I use this
device often, for realism. People don't always talk in neat, stage
like conversations.

The next common, and important, device is 'insert', particularly in
the modern era of computer screens and cell phone faces being,
well, inserted into films. So, you see the example here, as well as
its return to the scene. If you're insert is the end of a scene, you
can leave out 'back to scene', and simply start the next slug line.

Our last little tidbit for this chapter, the (cnt'd) at the bottom of a
page only when the scene is continuing, giving the cast and crew
some warning that there is more to the scene.

NINE

Had some fun clacking away? Fantastic. Let's talk about 'packaging up' your script. Yes, your 'book' WILL be judged by its cover. Even if forwarded electronically. The example is at the end of this chapter.

The wrapper of this package is literally your cover page. DO NOT try to flower this thing up! No color, no large print, no logos, no graphics. Nada. Also, use only white paper. If you feel that you need to ACTUALLY make a cover, use white card stock. Only white. Anything else says amateur. So, what's included? The title, in all caps, 'by', and your name. These items are centered. At the bottom of the page, right justified, is your contact info. Your name yes, again, address, phone, and email. That's it. Really.

Very important point comin' at you right away. A do-able script is about 100-120 pages. No one will even look at anything over 130, and you really don't want to be under 90.

A page is about a minute of screen time, roughly, so 120 is a full two hours, and a movie that is two hours plus is a LONG movie. Time for my soapbox. There are trained screenwriters out there scrapping for a chance to get their scripts into the hands of executives that they work right down the hall from. THEY are conforming to the three act, less than 120 page rule. If you are not, you have an even worse chance then they do, right? Think about it. Lecture over.

Okay, stay with me. Part of your conforming package is the application of some #4A brads. They're harder to find than you might think! (unless you live in Hollywood or Studio City) With a plain old three hole punch you will make the appropriate holes, and insert and flatten the tangs on these brads. Do I need to get on my soapbox again? I didn't think so. Conform. Conform, at this stage in your career.

Scripts that are actually made into movies go through a progression. They start as 'selling scripts', which are used to raise interest, then go through revisions, then eventually will become 'shooting scripts'.

Now, which kind of script do you think we should be working on at this point? You are correct, the selling script, because, as I mentioned in episode one, you will be 'selling' your cast and crew on working on your no or low budget set, even if you are not trying to actually sell the script to a studio. DON'T let someone who thinks they know about 'the game' talk you into inserting scene numbers, camera angles, and the like at this point. These are inappropriate at this point, and will make you look, wait for it, amateurish. Directors and cinematographers determine shots and angles. Not writers. Describe what is happening in your movie in the action, not with HELICOPTER SHOT'.

Script Types

Take a moment, please, and skim through this not real exciting but important topic. If one of us was to actually sell a screenplay to a studio, there would be a succession of different scripts, which would eventually make it to the point of the sides for a shooting day. These are usually attached to the back of the day's call sheet, and contain the dialogue for that day, no more, no less. These are usually printed half the size of a full size script, and are known for gigantic magic marker Xs slashed through whatever it being 'cut'.

Before that happened, the cast and key crew were given a 'shooting script'. This has scene numbers on it, which has now become important, as pre-production has to plan who has to show up where and when.

Different studios (and professional writers) have some other slight variations, but the earliest of the completed scripts is the version which you and I are now working to complete, and that is known as the 'selling script'. For good or for bad, the evening after you type THE END, and celebrate with an orange soda or two, the work really begins. As I've alluded to in the earlier parts of this witty tome, you will need to attract SOMEBODY with this screenplay. Agent, producer - actors and crew if you are producing; but you need to sell the idea that this is a worthwhile project. So, this version of the script needs to *read well.*

No scene numbers is the biggest difference. I would also encourage you to go a bit long with your character descriptions. The readers will probably try to mow through it in one sitting, they will need your help to imagine the 'movie'. Instead of:

MARIE, 26, tall and thin, entered the room.

Go for:

MARIE, 26, two shades from being translucent, and a full six foot in heels, glided through the door.

Why not do the same with your location descriptions? Paint the picture.

JIM AND SHEENA: A LOVE STORY

BY

TOM KENNERLY

WGA Registration #12341234

Tom Kennerly
1234 Main st.
Beaumont, PA 12345
717-555-1212
tkennerly@wahoo.com

See chapter sixteen for more on WGA registration, copyright, and the like.

TEN

Indie film producing. I could write a book on the subject...

...In 'No Budget Film Making', the path to making a feature film for a few dollars in such a way that you should be able to get distribution is discussed at length. That book does not cover script writing or directing, which led me to create this particular gem. This chapter is a place holder of sorts to let you know, if it isn't ridiculously obvious, that some type of work needs to happen in between typing 'THE END' and yelling ACTION. That work is called producing.

Producing is simply collecting the many and varied elements that are necessary for the production of a feature film; Actors, crew, locations, cameras, script, director, etc. A lot of folks think that Producers are the 'moneymen', that is a specific type of producer, an Executive Producer, or EP.

If I could briefly share with you a glimpse into my twisted mind, I started down the no-budget path by looking at the list in the previous paragraph by saying to myself, 'self, what if I got the actors to work for nothing, or almost nothing, what if I paid a DP to bring his own camera, and gave him just enough to make the next payment on it, what if I talked crew into working for free...'

You get the idea. If you collect a small group of you, and try to share these duties, it's even better. But, I digress, the point of this chapter is that, to get from script to yelling action, you must either:

- know how to produce;
- talk someone how knows how to produce into producing;
- buy a book on how to produce indie films;
- but my book on how to produce a no budget film.

I think that's a fair list of options.

Now, let's shoot this sucka...

ELEVEN

Let's discuss the basics of how to direct, by giving you the call signals that are used on actual Hollywood sets, thereby allowing you to control the chaos which is upward of a dozen people doing a dozen different things.

How do I know this works? It was not so long ago that I gathered a cast and crew for my first feature film, including a tiny bit of funding. At noon on the first day, we were ready. Everyone looked at me. Well?' I copied the things that I'd heard directors bark when I was an extra, and low and behold, it worked. So, copy me; you'll be fine.

In all my books I allude to the fact that the best movie makers are project managers. They organize their minds into groups of tasks, and have those tasks build to a 'sub goal'. Well, the sub goal that this chapter is about will prepare you to yell that classic word which has echoed across the back lot for decades; **Action.**

Let's construct the first sequence.

'Ready on the set'

This is a preliminary call. It simultaneously means, quiet, settle in, stop your adjustments, and 'tell me now if something's wrong'. Can also be **set,** or **setting** for short. At this point everyone will know that prep time is over.

'Camera'

You are checking or telling your camera operator to start recording, or continue, if for some reason he already is. He will respond with 'rolling', of course.

'Sound'

This call is necessary if you are not just using 'camera sound, which is a mike run out of the camera itself. You have a separate sound recording device that will later be synched. Your sound man will reply with 'sound speeding' or 'speeding'. I prefer speeding. Keep this in mind; despite all of the complications, cast and crew members, multiple locations, and million things that can go wrong, if you have a recording sound system, and a recording camera, you're making a movie.

'Background'

This cues everything that is NOT your speaking principles for the scene, starting their movement. This list includes extras, vehicles, props, set sound, snow, wind, or rain makers, anything that should be in motion BEFORE the first word of the first line of the scene. This is your chance, director, to make sure that you don't blow a good take. You want to let it unfold for a full second or two and make sure that exactly what you want is happening.

'Action'

Alright! You're about to 'get one'. Tip: If you're on a budget set, and dealing with cast and crew with little or no experience. You will have blown takes by people who don't wait for action, especially at the beginning of the day/scene/shoot. The tip is, I stretch out my call into one long sentence, Background, aaannnndddd, Action. They won't talk over you, so they won't 'go' too soon. So;

'Background and Action'

Alright, the actors do a great job with their lines, there are no interruptions, and you got a great take. It's finally time for you to bark out:

'Cut' (or cutting)

This comment is more technique than a basic but I'm throwing it in for free. At the moment that you are satisfied that the scene has reached its conclusion, wait for two beats. (In 'the game', it's not a 'second', it's a 'beat'.) Why do we wait? Primarily, editing. Your editor is linking all of the components of your masterpiece together, remember? He will need some overlap, or 'tail'. Remember how we called background and then action? This gave us some 'lead' for the same purpose. So, we have now waited a beat or two and **cut**.

So, ready to go get some coffee? Wait a minute, don't forget, every one is looking at you for DIRECTION. Several things could happen here. We'll look at the most common, so come back to them as you need to.

'Going again'

or

'Back to One'

or

'Resetting'

Simply means that everyone should reset to get another take of the same scene from the same angle. (by the way, 'back to one' derives from the actors being asked to return to their 'first position' in the scene.)

Twelve

More Directing Signals

The last chapter gave you the basics that will be repeated over and over, all day long. Here are a few that will help streamline the conversation. $10,000,000 budget or $500 budget, there's no need to waste time.

Turning Around

This means, same scene, DIFFERENT angle, probably the reverse, as in a conversation with alternating over the shoulder (OTS) shots.

Moving on

Can be interpreted in different ways, but I use it to say that we have finished that scene, and are moving on in the script, but we will not be moving from this general area.

New Set Up

or

New Deal

This means that the crew ARE moving. It could be thirty feet, it could be thirty miles, but they need a need to re set camera, lights, etc.

Picking Up

Sometimes it is not necessary to go all the back to 'from the top' which, as you can tell, I don't use. You will instruct your cast and crew how far back to go. Example:

"Picking up from, 'I hate you', Picking up *action*."

Hearing the director say 'picking up' is a cue for the post crew that they aren't 'missing something' when they find only part of the scene, if you have a script supervisor, they will note that this is a pick up, NOT a new take. To do this correctly you will already have to have said...

Continue the roll

Continue the roll is an alternative to cut. It allows you to briefly cue or adjust the cast, without causing a new take, or asking the crew to stop/start. Only used for a very brief instruction, like 'picking up from' or:

Example: Continue the roll, Annabeth, a little more volume please, and continuing *action*.

That's a Wrap

What a great feeling to say this!. This happens at the end of each day, not just at the end of the picture. ALSO, when an actor is finished with their part for the day, they are 'wrapped', and released. (for the day)

Only more exciting than yelling these things out on set will be when you get to the big time, where the director just sits in his chair frowning, and the First Assistant Director, or first AD does all of the barking. You'll be there one day.

THIRTEEN

How To Direct

In the first days of commercial motion picture production, The director was not considered to be a very important position. Over the course of motion picture history, that has changed to the point that the phrase 'at the helm' is used. Additionally, there are as many different types of directors as there are (complete your own metaphor).

I'm doing to tell you I one sentence how to direct, and you're not going to like it, but it's true. **Move your way through the script, without missing anything, in a way that lets the post production team assemble a feature film.**

That's it. If you use your own ears and eyes, it's a large step in the right direction. A set of headphones and a remote monitor have become really, really cheap – I know that this is not a technical book, but file that away to discuss with your cinematographer and sound guy or girl.

The Boring Truth

At the indie level the primary job of the director is to keep the production moving. You are truly the showrunner. Conserve your energy, as you will find that, like a parent, as soon as you turn your back, the machine starts to breakdown. If you were a team sports person, channel your coach during practice. Let's keep it moving, quick like a bunny, quickly now, going again right away; these phrases are called out all over the lots of southern California, and saying them without screaming is a skill to hone. I shoot my features in less than ten days, and you can bet that I have to keep it moving all day every day.

Let Your People Contribute

You hired these actors and actresses because of who they are. Same with your cinematographer. Give them a chance to do their thing, then guide them. I force myself to keep my mouth shut until I see one full take. You never know what someone else' interpretation may contribute to the project. Making movies is a group activity, and these artists will surprise you from time to time in fantastic ways if given a chance. And you'll get praise for being a great director, anyway!

You'll find your style. I think it's just as important to discuss what to avoid.

FOURTEEN

Three by Fives

This chapter can really, really, make the difference in production value for your indie film. This little system of mine is a half step toward story boarding, and I believe that it's the right thing to do at the no budget/severe low budget level.

Storyboarding, with a budget, is a series of artist's renderings that moves through the film in preproduction so that problems and opportunities can be identified by the key personnel. Why does this not work in no budget film making? One, because the budget that the studio has for storyboarding is greater than the budget for your whole film, and two, you have five thousand other things to do as writer/director/producer.

In fact, when I hear that an indie crew is getting into a storyboard situation, a red flag goes up. Why do they have the time and money for this? Storyboarding and table reads make me VERY suspicious at the no budget level, as it sounds like something you're doing to keep busy. If you have less than half a million dollars in budget, traditional story boarding is not something that I recommend. I'm not joking. Also, if you're reading this book, I'm guessing that you have a lot less than $500,000 slotted for your budget.

So, as promised, here is how to but the 'good' of storyboarding to use for your project, without the financial or time strain. Get yourself a ninety-nine cent packet of three by five cards, and a rubber band. While the nerds are poking through their tablets at the coffee shop, you start doing a small, rough sketch of your favorite scenes on these cards, one at a time. You can start with your favorites, and work out of order, filling in as much of the movie as you can. In a corner of each card, you will nickname the scene (Jim and Sheena drive to the country), and note the location and characters needed. You can carry this packet around with you and do a few at a time, taking your time to picture the location, key action, and mood.

The artistic reason for doing this is that it is the film maker's job to fill the screen with entertainment, and each of the cards should have something to say to you as you complete them, while simultaneously moving the plot along. The practical reason for doing this, young film maker, is that you are ironing out the 'reality' of shooting this film. 'Jim and Sheena drive to the country'. Do you and or your DP know how to capture images at sixty five miles an hour in a moving vehicle, and have the equipment to do so?

These cards will make it all the way to the first day of shooting, and you will be the exceptional indie film maker as you refer back to them, and direct the cast and crew with what you have already perceived in your mind's eye.

FIFTEEN

Roadblocks

As you find your own style, you can do your best to steer away from these common problems, and I will have absorbed some of the pain for you, as, I've made every mistake there is, trust me.

Love Interest

Okay, I didn't make this mistake personally. Not that my leading ladies weren't desirable. But I **was** recruited for a film that stopped and started twice, and both times, the film maker had cast his GF in a lead or key crew role. Two different girls, mind you. Haven't heard from him since the second tank. Don't do it. At the ten million dollar level, you can have a tiff or a breakup, and everybody still comes to work because they have Ferrari payments. Not so in no and low budget. You've been warned.

Self Deprecation

First, I can't believe that I know how to spell deprecation. Seriously, I was so thrilled to have the cameras rolling on my first feature, that I was a bit of a mouse and a pushover. For the first two days. When things started going off course, I roared, and we almost lost the script supervisor. Start and stay fair but firm. These people are on the set because they needed to be part of a project, and they needed you to lead them. Don't cut down anyone, including yourself.

Directing By Committee - Unsolicited Input

I like to say that in all areas of business, committees rarely approve bad ideas, but they also rarely approve good ideas. If Deniro is on your set, take his input. Anyone less accomplished than him, you're not interested. A film production is a train ride, and if you change direction in the middle, you just ain't gonna get where you're going. I hate to preach, but this is one reason that you want a strong script with direction laid out in black and white. (this comment applies to post production too, by the way)

Here's one great way to keep your cast feeling like you DO listen to them: The actor suggests a different line or action. You follow up with, "Okay, tell you what. Let's do one the way it's written, then one your way. We'll see how the camera likes it." Anyone who won't go along with this, is just a prima donna.

SIXTEEN

This chapter is technical, so I put it toward the back. In this chapter we will review the types of shots that need to happen so that a scene can be created by your editor. You've seen them all before, you just didn't know their technical terminology. Let's revisit Jim and Sheena:

INT. JIM'S KITCHEN - NIGHT

Sheena and Jim look at their hands as they sit across from each other at the kitchen table.

           SHEENA
    I'm sorry, Jim, I shouldn't have...

           JIM
        (stepping on)
    No, no, it was my fault.

Sheena and Jim stretch their hands across the table, and both smile as they hold each others hands tightly.

INSERT - Jim's cellphone VIBRATES on the kitchen table.

                        (cnt'd)

```
BACK TO SCENE

                    SHEENA
          Oh boy, I know who that is.


                                        FADE
```

A very typical scene – two folks talking at a table. Here is what I see:

A **Master:** The table at the bottom of the frame, both of their profile in full.

Over the shoulder (OTS): Over Jim's shoulder for Sheena's line, over Sheena's for Jim's.

Extreme Close Up (ECU): The phone vibrates.

Master: The phone vibrates.

You will shoot the whole scene, especially as this is a very short one, from each of these angles. This allows the editors the flexibility to pick the exact right moment to cut to and away. For instance, to add a bit of foreshadowing, he may show the phone doing nothing in between their mutual apologies.

Deciding that you 'don't need something' is called editing in the camera, and won't allow your editor as much flexibility. Indie film makers have tough choices in this area, as you need to keep the show moving, but more angles equals better production value without a doubt. Your job is to strike a balance.

More Shots:

Two Shot: two people on screen at the same time, usually between bust and ¾ length

Close Up: Just as it sounds.

POV: From the point of view of the character.

You can come up with s shot list the night before, or the morning of, if you have the time. Your cinematographer will love you for it. Otherwise, the two of you will review this as you move to your new setup, and the crew can 'set' after you agree on what the two of you want to 'get'. Less professional, but if you're the writer/director/producer, sometimes that's the way it's gotta be.

SEVENTEEN

Copyright

Boring but important, here is another resource chapter. If you're intending to produce or coproduce your script, you will have to start making it available to your potential cast and crew, probably via email, to gain their buy in. Some of you may be wondering, ' what if they run off and...

...the odds of someone taking your script, excluding you, and finishing a film, are so remote, that you should be more worried about an asteroid hitting earth. You will realize this after you make your OWN film, believe me.

However, it's worth the time protecting your work for other reasons. Should you produce your own film and sell it, the script needs to be copyrighted. Should you pitch the idea to an investor or a studio, it needs to be registered. Note, I said pitch, not buy. It needs to be registered with WGO or the copyright office just for them *to look*.

So, here are some basics. The two ways to register/protect your script are with the US Copyright Office, and WGA, the Writer's Guild. They can both be done online, in fact online registration is encouraged. Both organizations want your cash, of course. The WGA is a faster process if you suddenly come across an opportunity to submit your script and you've put off registration. The copyright registration last longer (with a few minor exceptions, until you croak). Consider, if you are writing this script, and know that you will be producing the film and then marketing it, you may as well go with the copyright office, as your distribution partner will want the script copyrighted, the WGA registration will probably not be enough.

So why go with WGA at all? Frankly, your script could be hanging around within the marketing stage for a looooong time, before being produced and sold, and WGA is a quick, easy option. Your choice, here are the links.

www.wgawregistry.org

www.copyright.gov

One final comment; about copyright; technically, you are protected by copyright law without registering. We all are here in the US. So, in the formative stages of your script, one shouldn't be biting one's fingernails worrying about theft. However, as piracy in the latter stages of distribution becomes more and more common, having that registration date with your name is a clear anchor in what will become the 'chain of title' of your project.

EIGHTEEN

What do you want to do with your film?

I see you. I can see you right now. There is a big uhhhh forming behind your teeth. Very common. Let me guess at a few inklings crossing your mind regarding the possible future of your film:

- I want people to see it,
- Film Festivals, I guess,
- Find a producer's rep – whatever that is...
- OK, I'll say it, fame and fortune!

I've been there, so I apologize for the sarcasm. However, you need to decide what you want to do with your film. It really, really, will affect the type of film that you make and how you make it. If you've made it this far, I can assume that you want to commercially distribute your film, but you may have just assumed that all feature length films are eventually commercially distributed. Not true at all. *Most feature length films do not achieve a commercial distribution deal.* Period. The majority of films that *show at Sundance* do not achieve a commercial distribution deal. Now that's scary.

What would one do with a feature length film that is finished? Let's briefly discuss some options:

1) You could have a blast entering in into film festivals that want your type of film. You could get into larger festivals that are attended by industry folks, get noticed, and be asked to pitch them your next idea or script.

2) You could show it at local independent theatres, with whom you would pay a flat fee and then sell tickets to your friends, relatives, fans, etc. This is called 'four-walling' in the industry. You can even invite local press, but you know that there won't be anyone there from the 'studios' because you would have to have invited them.

3) You can stream it on the internet, in an increasingly wide variety of low and no cost scenarios. At this writing I know not one person who has made a buck doing this, but I know people who have had a ton of 'hits'. Basically a youtube.com style of exposure. Quick: What's your favorite web series? Yeah...

4) Look for a distribution partner. There will be little or no upfront money, you will probably have to throw your own premiere, and you will wait for months (at least) until you see it available for sale, but this is just about the only way that you have

a shot at international distribution or national cable distribution. This was my goal, as the rest of this rambling diatribe suggests. This is the step to the big time. Film Festivals are just another form of self marketing. Four walling is another form of self marketing.

5) Don't worry about it. Argh! I told you, I'm a planner. I don't believe that making a film, and THEN deciding what to do with it is good business, but at least reading this has put the end game in your head.

A quick comment about Producer's Reps: If you have been doing research, the true producer's rep is not as prevalent as he or she once was. Anyone who is not a distributor who says that he wants the exclusive right to market your film needs to REALLY explain to you why he should be given that exclusive right. That explanation should include past successes. It just doesn't make sense that he could pull this off and not consider himself to be either a distributor or a producer. Be cautious. Some folks love the film industry and enjoy matchmaking at this level for a few bucks here and there, but the snakes that have hung around the industry have given them all a mediocre reputation.

I have a chapter very similar to this one in my other books, and as they are producer oriented, I place them early on. I wanted to do the artist in you a favor, and put this practical thinking toward the end, letting you get a creative head of steam going before slapping you in the face with reality. I'll end this chapter with an old man sounding summary: If you know where you're planning to go with this project, you have a much better chance of getting there...

In Conclusion

Debating is rampant in the entertainment business because there is probably no other industry which can match it's unemployment level, so cast and crew alike meet in coffee shops and tell each other 'how to make it'. Don't you fall prey to this, unless you're really bored and want some cheap entertainment. However your project gets into distribution is the 'how' of how to make it. Don't let anyone tell you otherwise, including me.

A cliché way of debating whether someone is on the right path or not, is to break up the phrase Show Business into its two components, show and business. "Well, it is a business," says the producer, when he asks if his niece, who was a theatre major, can run the auditions, before he will hand over your much needed funds. "I need a rewrite, then we'll talk money," says another producer. Is he just stalling for time, repeating something he overheard at another meeting, or did he spot a typo on every other page, and wants you to get your act together?

One of the chief reasons I put the 'No Budget' books together is to give ALL of us a choice. You can leave the coffee shop debating to the wannabes, and start making your movie. Right or wrong, you have the option of doing it yourself on a shoe string, and telling producers, their nieces, and girlfriends, that you'll 'pass'.

See you on the red carpet...

DEFINITIONS

Abbey Singer – The next to the last shot on a shoot day. Abbey Singer was a crew member who consistently called out 'martini', the actual last shot, prior to the actual last shot. Hey, she's better known on Hollywood sets than other crew members, and almost all actors...

AD – Assistant Director.

Background – As a noun, a professional term for extras. Also a command, as shots involving extras will have 'background' called before 'action'.

Bounce Board – A silver coated, lightweight board used to reflect light onto a specific portion of a shot. Bounce boards are used at all budget levels, but are a particular must have for the indie film maker.

C47 – A term meant to haze newbies and give light entertainment to crew members on long days, a c-47 is simply code for an everyday household clothespin. You read it here.

CCM – Short for copy, credit, meals.

Copy, Credit, Meals – The way in which no and low budget film makers frequently compensate cast and crew for their time and services. Copy is short for copy of the film, credit is the fact that you will be credited in the films titles or end credits, and meals, of course, that you will be fed something, probably high carb, while on set.

Costume Party – A period piece in which a considerable amount of the budget goes into wardrobe and other related art department spending.

Craft Service – Smart film makers at every level keep the cast and crew working by having water, coffee, other beverages, and snack items available on set at all times. The first time somebody leaves the set to run for coffee, and three others put in an order, and then two others go along for the ride, will be the last time you shoot without craft service. The name is derived from this service being a requirement of the various 'craft' guilds and unions on union projects.

Crafty – short for Craft Service.

DP – the Director of Photography, or cinematographer. This is the guy who really studied, light, motion, color, and perspective, and lends his artistic expertise as such.

Development – Of the five stages which comprise film production at any level, development is the first.

Digital Intermediate – In order for the powerful and multi featured digital editing software programs to be used on true film footage, this footage must be turned into digital files for editing to occur. A print (or negative) may then be struck by converting the digital cut back into film, or analog state. Hence the intermediary digital stage, or, digital intermediate.

EP – Executive Producer. The money man!

First – usually 'The First'. The first assistant director. On medium to large sets, the director will be behind his monitor scratching his chin, while the first is out pushing and barking.

Five and Dimed – not heard much these days, but a favorite of the author's. Process in which someone reads the first five and last ten (dime) pages of the script, so that if asked, they can converse as if having read the whole thing. (Don't five and dime me on this one, Horst.)

Holding – Mainly for extras, but a place where anyone who is not involved in filming at that particular time can be held, far enough away so that noise does not affect the shooting, but close enough so that they can be brought in immediately after the First AD screams for them.

Honeywagon – A portable trailer that that holds the self contained bathrooms for location shooting. May also contain the dressing rooms for lower than star level actors/extras.

In – The DP, first camera, or first AD, or any combination of these will look through the camera after the shot is set, and make sure that things that are not supposed to be 'in' the camera's frame are not, and that things that are supposed to be 'in', are in fact 'in'.

Martini – The last shot of the filming day.

Mechanical – A mechanical is even 'rougher' than a rough cut, and is the first assembly of what was shot during production following the script from being to end.

MUA – Abbreviation for makeup artist.

Out – Out of frame. Q: "Should I move that plant?" A: "Don't worry, it's out."

P and A – Stands for Prints and Advertising.

Prints and Advertising – Once a film is finished, the minimum cost of going into theatrical distribution was known as the cost of prints and advertising; the cost of the film copies combined with the advertising to support the film can easily rival the cost of the film itself. Note: Digital 'prints' have lowered this cost dramatically.

Pancake – a small box, usually part of a set, used for raising equipment just a bit.

PA – Production Assistant. the PA is the low man on the totem pole on the set, and the variety of things they are ordered to do expand and contract with the needs and complexity of the set.

Post – Post production. Everything that goes into the final cut after principal photography has wrapped.

Pre – Pre-production. After being green lit, the organization of a project so as to get into production.

Principle – short for 'principle character'. A lead role.

Producer – The are many types of producers in the game. A definition that I have used that stands up over time is that a producer's job is to acquire all of the resources with which to produce a film or video project.

Screener – A complimentary or promotion copy of a film for the purpose of promotion or review.

Script Supervisor – This person sits at a desk like station with a small light onset, and follows the script for the rest of the cast and crew, remaining as true to the shooting script as possible. The script is also usually responsible for the shot reports.

Scripty – Slang for script supervisor.

Slate – Several meanings. 1) The clapper has changed quite a bit over time, but used to be a small chalkboard or slate, now usually a combination of dry erase and digital. 2) during auditions, 'slating' means looking at the camera at the beginning of the audition, and stating your name, character you are reading for, etc. 3) Producers or showrunners consider the projects that they have in the pipeline at any given time to be their 'slate'.

Showrunner – When someone is a combination star and producer of a sitcom or movie, or perhaps writer/director/producer or a movie. Everyone else 'gets in line with' the showrunner.

Stinger – Piece of electrical equipment that allows for the input of several lights.

Supporting – Usually used as 'supporting role'. A character that has significant screen time, but is still not a lead.

Theatrical – The Holy Grail. Studios are designed to plan for theatrical distribution, but Indie Film Makers consider this winning the lottery. This means that your film is replicated into multiple prints, and put into a number of theatres at one time. the term would usually apply to this happening domestically.

VOD – Video on demand.

Waiver – There are many types, but if you sign one, you are giving up your rights, or 'waiving' your rights, for example, to future compensation.

ABOUT THE AUTHOR

Tom Kennerly lives with his pet fish in Camp Hill, Pennsylvania. He publishes fact and fiction, purely based on his mood.

Also By Tom Kennerly

No Budget Film Making

The Two Roomer

The Happy Caterpillars

Fraternal

Swag

Model Citizen

www.ingramcontent.com/pod-product-compliance
Lightning Source LLC
Chambersburg PA
CBHW051347170526
45166CB00002B/999